Building Blocks

for the *NEW* Retirement

An easy, interactive 8-step
guide for a retirement
with meaning, purpose
and fun

By Joan Tabb

Author of *Great in Eight: Job Seeking Skills*

Dedicated to my sister Amy:

The happiest and most engaged retired
person I've ever seen

Table of Contents

Introduction

Dear Reader,

Congratulations! You are a pioneer, heading into new territory where few have gone before. By 2020 more than 20 percent of the population in the United States will be over the age of 65. This aging of the population is occurring in many parts of the world. It means millions of people, for the first time in history, will have the time to pursue decades of vital years ahead.

My mission with this book is to have you bring your best to this exciting new stage of life. This stage has been called 'retirement' for decades, but many of us don't like that term anymore. We associate it with being outside the mainstream of life. I personally prefer a term like 'revitalment' that includes the vitality that many of us bring to our later years. For the sake of being easily understood I use the word 'retirement' in this book and add on the New to describe a different way we can be in our later years.

Many of you will bring:
- good enough health
- good enough financial security (perhaps semi-retired or working part-time)
- and hopefully decades ahead of time to fill

The big question is:
How do you best fill that gift of time?

This book gives you an easy, eight step, multi-faceted guide that is interactive and fun. It's about self-discovery and formulating a vision for the New Retirement that is unique and customized to your life. Although multi-faceted, this book does not include the topic of managing your finances. Many other resources cover that topic thoroughly.

Using best practices in adult learning, the approach is relevant and efficient. You are presented with a concept, then asked to apply it to your life. At the end of each chapter is *Your Turn*, which presents probing questions and creative exercises.

Each chapter includes examples from real people interviewed for this book; some who might be similar to you in their experiences and insights. Their stories might prompt you to think of your own.

Let's harvest your rich life—lessons learned, interests, values and insights. You will rediscover gems of yourself that may have been forgotten along the way. Readers have especially enjoyed Chapter 7, Exploring the New, where you consider new directions.

There are eight building blocks or topics, and in the last one you create your own *Action Plan*, based on your discoveries along the way. My hope with this book is to invigorate dynamic people like you with something as simple and profound as building blocks.

I invite you to start your journey. The best is yet to come. Let's bring the best of you to the New Retirement!

Onward,

Joan

CHAPTER ONE

In the Beginning

Reclaiming your childhood interests

Setting the Stage

In our society we are conditioned to be responsible and hard working. We are rewarded for achievement and success, seeing ourselves being graded as A or B students, for example or as workers earning a certain income. These are measures that have come to us from the outside. We are not accustomed to being inner-directed.

Naturally, many of us continue to be outer-focused as we face our retirement years. Once we have taken care of our responsibilities, provided for our families, and our financial future, we still look to society to tell us how to live. These past models reflected a different reality; before people were as healthy and vital as we are. *I'm suggesting that now, as pioneers, we journey into new terrain and take the time to build new models for our new age of retirement.*

> "What did you do as a child that made the hours pass like minutes? Therein lies a key to your essential self."
>
> —Carl Jung

Society offers us limited models of success for later years. For many generations retirement lasted only a year or two before they died. They worked until they were worn out. In contrast, we now may have decades of vitality after our work life ends. We see images of people playing golf, traveling, and enjoying grandchildren. We hear of retirees focusing time and resources on restoring their youthful appearance. Those activities are fine, but we can do more!

In our *new* retirement we have the luxury of time to re-visit and explore our deeper selves. We need to pause and reflect on our nature. We have lived many decades and have accumulated wisdom, experience, skills, insights and resources. We can now operate from our essential selves. We can peel back from the demands of society to our personal preferences and ideas of fun and enjoyment before the demands of being an adult kicked in.

Let's begin by taking a look at early ourselves from the inside-out.

"There is tremendous value in going from the inside-out to truly own and wisely navigate your life forward."

—Joan Tabb

Research shows that our deep nature remains the same lifelong. If you were a bookworm who adored time alone to read, you probably still have that connection to solitude and the life of the mind. If you were a child who relished time with friends, you probably still have a desire for a rich social life. It's good to know our nature.

This is your chance to examine your life and connect the dots that really make you who you are. Then you can choose what to do with your freedom and time, to *intentionally* shape the decades ahead.

What comes to mind when you are asked to think about your happiest memories of childhood? Do you think of the warmth of family, time with a pet, playing with friends, enjoying school? Perhaps you think of time alone reading a book or looking up at cloud formations. Maybe it's about sports and playing ball or skiing. Maybe you felt loved and cared for as you prepared meals with your mother. Perhaps you think of school and topics that fascinated you that you never had a chance to explore.

Often the things that delighted us most as children reveal our essence—our true selves. Due to circumstances and life pressures, we often get away from that essential self.

Let's Look Back at Your Childhood

Let's examine the temperament, preferences and style that were you before the demands of school, peer pressure, career and other factors influenced your life. Let's identify aspects of your early self so you can extract meaningful nuggets and use them to build your future.

What memories bring a smile to your face? What made deep and positive impressions on you?

Self-awareness is the first step in constructing a purposeful and vital retirement.

Tammy—The Book Lover

Tammy was a serious child who loved to read. In school she was bright in all subjects and cherished library time with hundreds of volumes, new stories, and ideas all around her. Raised in Texas, she was encouraged to become a petroleum engineer.

She liked her profession, but it was very demanding. Between work and family obligations she had little time for her number one passion, reading.

She knew that whatever she did in retirement, it must provide time for her to read and be around books. Tammy finally retired as an engineer and made good on her never forgotten love of reading. She is now the owner of a bookstore in her adopted state of Wyoming, with her son as assistant. He is another book lover who inherited the same love of words.

Alex—The Horse Lover

Let's look at Alex anticipating his retirement and looking back on his life.

Alex's best childhood memories are of riding horses on the coast of Argentina where he grew up. He has many happy memories of summers at his cousin's ranch, away from the city. All during the school year he would fantasize about being back in the saddle, riding and taking care of the horses.

He remembers the smells, the sounds, the wind and his deep connection to a special horse. The smile on his face is a mile wide as he relates the joy he felt in cantering on the beach and feeling free and happy. Fast forward, his life turned out to have many challenges. His family moved to the United States and he was promptly drafted into the Vietnam War. He used the GI Bill to get his education and spent most of his life focused on work. His first wife died young and he had a lot of responsibilities raising his children solo.

At 64 he retired in good health. Finally, with time on his hands and a comfortable retirement he now had the time to think about how to use *free time*, something that was rare for him in the decades prior to his retirement.

He knows that horses and riding need to play a major role in his life going forward.

Sam—The PhD Performer

Sam was a mimic and a singer from the time he was a toddler. He just loved to act, sing, dance and perform for anyone who'd take the time to watch. He was also a very intelligent and precocious child who taught himself to read at the age of three. His intellectual capabilities were

shown early on as he loved math and science. He was greatly rewarded for his talents and academic achievements.

He grew up in a working class family and they were delighted to have a first child recognized for his intellect. He was offered a full scholarship to college and he became an engineer.

But he always had the performer in him! Finally, in his mid-60's, upon retirement, he decided to reawaken that passion and his local community theater was delighted to have his contributions.

Fran–Finally with Her Pets and Animals

"Find out where joy resides, and give it a voice beyond singing. For to miss the joy is to miss all."

—Robert Louis Stevenson

Fran was a child who delighted in bringing home stray pets. She adored animals, begged her parents for a pet, but they pointed to the apartment building rules that did not allow animals. She had a lot of responsibilities as a child and knew she'd need to take care of herself in life.

She became a bookkeeper, later a CPA, and she had to ignore her early yearning for animals. Approaching retirement, as she probed her childhood memories, she became aware of that early love. It sparked deep, powerful and positive associations so she decided to act on it. Now she is an active volunteer at her local humane society. Plus, she lives with both a rescue cat and dog.

Self-awareness is the first step in constructing a purposeful and vital retirement.

YOUR TURN:

1. What brought you joy as a child? What were favorite and fun activities? What other positive things do you recall about yourself as a child? What were your dreams and hopes as a child?

_____

_____

_____

_____

2. Are there activities and passions you enjoyed that had to come to an end due to life circumstances? (This can be painful. For Alex, he remembered being sad and disappointed when his family moved to the US. There was no longer access to the ranch or to horseback riding)

_____

_____

_____

3. Write a short narrative about yourself in the style of the ones in this chapter? Remember Tammy the book lover or Sam the performer? Try to write a piece describing yourself as a child.

_____

_____

_____

_____

_____

_____

_____

_____

_____

CHAPTER TWO

Your One Body

Care for it, appreciate it

You were only given one body for this lifetime. It requires more maintenance and care as we age. Many of us didn't have to pay too much attention to the body until our later decades.

There's the physical to consider and there's the aesthetic part. Sadly, our culture sees an aging face as bad and undesirable. It is not just how our body works that worries us, but how we think our body appears to others.

Some in their 50s or older, confide that sometimes when they see themselves in a mirror or an unplanned selfie, they are shocked and aghast. They see an aging face, a paler one, with some lines and furrows, perhaps less hair. We miss our youthful looks. It's natural to miss the beauty of youth. But sadly, our culture does not seem to value the different kind of inside-out, deeper beauty of age.

> "I believe that exercise is the key not only to physical health but to peace of mind."
>
> —Nelson Mandela

One reason we feel the shock when we look into a mirror or at a photo is because on the inside we still feel like we are youthful. My mother up until her late 80s said that on the inside she remained a girl of 16. Her approach was to stop looking in the mirror and to refuse to be photographed.

Our energy is still good, we still feel curious and healthy (most of the time). We feel attractive on the inside when we are interested in what's around us. We ignore the image of our aging until we are forced to recognize it. Instead of gratitude that we have so much of our youth inside, we try to reshape the outside.

When we study Rembrandt we learn that his self-portraits only get more interesting and actually more beautiful as he ages. We learn that in the Asian cultures, which value and respect the elderly, the smile lines and facial wrinkles are regarded as beautiful. Let's try to move more in that direction. I read that a smile takes 10 years off our appearance. In other words, find ways to feel good from the inside-out rather than the outside-in, and it will actually add to your appeal.

Lifelines

I have a new concept for us to consider. I call it *Lifelines*. The lines that form on our face reflect the lives we have lived. So, too, do lifelines reflect JOY! Friends of mine recently became grandparents and when I see their proud, happy faces as they hold their next generation I am aware of the lifelines of happiness on their faces.

A few months after I got over the initial shock of my mother's death after an unusually close and best friend relationship, the realization hit me powerfully that *death is real* and I would have my time to go, too.

I realized that the wheels of time and aging are inexorably moving forward; they cannot be stopped. But, what I can do is strengthen my body, build muscle, and create a more powerful physical stance. I could accept the lifelines forming on my face as a reaction to my deep loss and appreciate the richness of life expressed on my face, but I chose not to accept sitting by (literally) watching my body soften and age when I could do something about it. Two and a half years ago I joined a gym and started a three times a week strength-training regime. Now my body is stronger, my posture more upright, and I have gained an inner mind-body awareness with more confidence and discipline.

We can't fight the passage of time, but we can always create more strength, no matter when we start.

Activity

One of the reasons we are living longer is that we have medical and life-style advances that support longevity. As our bodies age, they typically do require more maintenance and care to allow us to have active lives.

Let's face it. We have older bodies and they are not at their peak. Typically, as we get into our 60s, 70s and 80s we have some health issues, perhaps some aches and pains. Fine, but we are still alive and ready. Let's find new ways to keep fit that don't involve as much pounding and effort.

Tom went from participating in marathons to shorter races with men in his age group. His competitive spirit was still engaged as he faced less competition with the 70-80 year-olds than he did when he was in his 20s-60s.

Research shows that moderate exercise, even walking three times a week regularly, can do a lot to keep us healthy. If we bring a friend or two along and add a social dimension, we add to its efficacy. In some cases, we need to make changes to our diets and our activities to remain strong and flexible.

I found that the most vibrant and happy people put a lot of time and attention into their physical well-being. It is the foundation of their overall well-being. For most of them, moderation was the key for both healthy diets and healthy activity levels. Those who once were

"Those who think they have no time for bodily exercise will sooner or later have to find time for illness."

—Edward Stanley

competitive athletes scaled down to less demanding sports. Susan went from competitive singles tennis to competitive pickleball, a sport that is far less rigorous but still can be played with vigor. Many people mention continuing to enjoy golf lifelong. It is a social sport, gets you outdoors and active, and it provides a challenge with each swing of the club.

If you haven't been active in years, or have limited mobility, you might still find ways to enhance your health; perhaps with easy walking or gentle swimming. Many community recreation centers and athletic clubs now offer exercise programs for seniors that accommodate physical limitations or chronic conditions.

Your Appearance

Society gives us powerful messages about how we're supposed to look. It tells us we must work to restore our youthful appearance. Why? Think about it. It doesn't take a cynic to see there clearly is an economic and marketing angle to this.

"I've had so much plastic surgery, when I die they will donate my body to Tupperware."

—Joan Rivers

Look at all the ways you can spend your time and money. *Do you really want to put a lot of it in the direction of your appearance?* Plastic surgeons, aesthetic dermatologists, cosmetic companies, all are trying to make a living off our desire to turn back the clock. I'm not suggesting you not look your best. But I am suggesting that it is a decision that comes from the inside-out rather than from advertising designed to provoke insecurity or invoke societal pressure.

Only you can answer how much is right for you. My goal is to make you conscious of your choices.

How much is enough? In my discussion with many contented retirees, I found that most of them have been tempted to have a better and more youthful appearance. We live in a youth-oriented culture and the messages to look younger are profound. The happiest ones made very careful and thoughtful decisions in this area.

Frank looked into hair replacement but realized that for the cost of the procedure, he could take his family on a two-week vacation. A family vacation would provide experiences and memories that were more powerful and significant for everyone—new hair on his head—not so much.

Eating and Drinking Habits

Diet is another area to address. Sadly, many of us cannot eat and drink like we did when we were younger. Research shows that those living in cultures who have the longest lives have healthier and more restrictive diets, not only in the older years but lifelong. The people in long-lived cultures also tend to eat in social groups, not alone. We'll talk about this more in Chapter Seven, Ya Gotta Have Friends.

> "The food you eat can be the safest and most powerful form of medicine or the slowest form of poison."
>
> —Ann Wigmore

People who enjoyed an evening of long dinners with rich foods, cocktails and wine, are now opting for smaller meals and limiting themselves to one or two drinks. Moderation is the key to taking care of our aging bodies. Unless you have diabetes or other illnesses, you can still enjoy the occasional birthday cake and evening out with rich foods. But doing it once in a while is a key to good health.

This is an area in which we need to be intentional, and tune into our bodies. If we do not listen to our bodies and change habits as needed we can lose our vigor. We all want to have the freedom to live our lives fully, by personal choice, as possible.

Other Health Considerations as We Get Older

Core—Without strength in our core, our stomach muscles and those that surround our critical organs, as one woman said, "Without core

strength I couldn't get up in the morning!" It's vital to exercise and keep that core strong.

Skin Protection—In retirement we tend to be outdoors more, so sunscreen is vital. We also need to moisturize our naturally dryer skin.

Water—Just when our bodies require more hydration the signals to our brain that we are thirsty, fade. We need to drink water regularly, even when we do not feel thirsty. Most visits to the ER among those 60 and over include dehydration.

Shoes/Clothing—Our bodies are changing. Our feet are our foundation and they now require more care. Most women said that they greatly reduced or eliminated wearing heels and opted for attractive flats with good support. Many women and men say that comfort now comes first, before fashion.

Rest/sleep—Many mentioned getting fatigued more quickly and that they require more rest and naps. Some people were concerned at first when they needed to awaken to urinate or just wake up for an hour or two. They learned to not panic and used that time to read or think. Falling asleep can become more difficult so you might need to learn new habits of relaxation, reduce screen time before bed, darken and reduce the sleeping environment or more.

It's paradoxical that the idea of living a long life appeals to everyone, but the idea of getting old doesn't appeal to anyone."

—Andy Rooney

Secrets of Longevity

When it comes to making it into your 90s, booze actually beats exercise, according to a long-term study. The research, led by University of California neurologist Claudia Kawas, tracked 1,700 nonagenarians. Researchers discovered that subjects who drank about two glasses of beer or wine a day were 18 percent less likely to experience a premature death.

Meanwhile, participants who exercised 15 to 45 minutes a day, cut the same risk by 11 percent. Subjects who kept busy with a daily hobby two hours a day were 21 percent less likely to die early, while those who drank two cups of coffee a day cut that risk by 10 percent.

Sandy—Opts for a Facelift

Sandy was delighted that her first child was getting married, but she was also depressed at the thought of her aging appearance at his wedding. She would be seeing many friends and family she hadn't seen in a long time and knew that her skin had wrinkled considerably. Her deep frown lines did not reflect her inner happiness and joy.

She decided she really wanted a facelift to look better at her son's wedding. She did it to please herself, and she was glad she had it done. She wanted to look great in the photographs and she did. But she made the decision to do it once, and then not invest more in her naturally aging face.

Susan—Hires a Trainer and Goes Off Botox

Susan was a corporate executive. She worked 60-80 hours a week and traveled throughout the country. Her work involved long business dinners and she often had little time for exercise. She was a typical weekend warrior, doing heavy workouts on the weekend and perhaps a round of golf. She enjoyed rich dinners but noticed a significant weight gain in her 50s. She decided it could not continue.

Her reaction was to hire a personal trainer who showed her how to fit workouts into her hectic life. She learned to do a 10 minute workout in her hotel room with weights and bands. She learned to add more walking: to use the stairs instead of escalators and walk rather than using the moving sidewalks in airports.

She also consulted with a nutritionist who suggested she employ smart eating. She began ordering two appetizers or an appetizer and a salad at the dinners and limiting her alcohol. She did all of this mindfully as she noted and respected the changes her body required to continue being strong, fit, and vital.

While Susan was at the corporation her key role was business development—the "rainmaker" that brought in new business. This involved regularly meeting people and being the 'face of the firm'. She knew that her aging appearance did not support the image of a vibrant, relevant firm, so for the last five years she was getting regular Botox injections to erase her wrinkles. Upon retirement, she felt free of the need to invest in a certain appearance and felt the money could be much better spent on fun and exciting life experiences, like travel, rather than on her face.

Mark—The Extra 30 Pounds

Mark, a small business owner facing retirement at 64, had been carrying an extra 30 pounds for the last 15 years. He kept promising himself and his wife that he'd take care of his weight as soon as he had the time to exercise. He was warned by his physician that with his weight gain and getting older, he was in a pre-diabetic state. Then work became more demanding. You get the picture. Mark was getting impatient with his health going downhill fast. He finally decided that he'd have no more excuses upon retirement.

Mark met with his physician, asked to be put on a reasonable and smart diet to address his pre-diabetic state. He decided that even though it was expensive, he'd invest in a personal trainer twice a week to really combine diet and exercise for long-term better health and enjoyment.

He realized that an early source of joy in his marriage had been hiking and he wanted to get back in shape by resuming hikes with his wife.

They had enjoyed hiking together back in their college and early family building years, but it had gone by the wayside. Now it was time to bring it back as a new and healthy hobby.

YOUR TURN

1. How are you taking care of your health? What are you doing well? What could be better? Are you up to date on any medical conditions? Do you need to see any health professionals?

_____

_____

_____

_____

_____

2. How do you feel about your changing body as you age? Weight concerns? Strength concerns? Do you need to address eating, drinking or sleeping habits? How will you change habits?

_____

_____

_____

_____

_____

3. How do you feel about your changing appearance as you age? Is there anything you'd consider changing? What research will you do? What is the trade-off for the time and money invested?

_____

_____

_____

_____

_____

CHAPTER THREE

Extracting from Your Career Life

Skills to bring forward?

What aspects of your working life might you want to bring forward into your retirement? Is this a building block for you?

Years ago, when you retired, you put in your 30 years and were gone, done. It was good bye to your work, to your career. One day you were fully engaged at work and the next day you were out the door. Often, the retiree was tired and glad to say goodbye to their working days. They were ready to spend that time rocking on the porch, playing golf or cards. They were worn out and typically died within a few years.

Those times are gone. Now many of us plan ahead for financial freedom and in our later decades, find ourselves vital and ready for more: more activity, more experiences, more enjoyment. The sources of your vitality may be coming from aspects of your career. If your career was raising a family, home management, or caregiving you too will be experiencing changes when the nest gets smaller or perhaps when you downsize. All of these activities gave us skills, paid or unpaid.

"The vision of people 55+ spending their retirement golfing and lounging by the beach is out. Meaningful work is in."

—Kerry Hannon

Maybe you want to continue using those skills. The new work might take a different form, not full time and perhaps not in a management or supervisorial role. I've found from interviewing and presenting this possibility, that many people still hold a fascination and enjoyment with parts of the work life they had before they moved into management. They welcome the opportunity to find ways to express and use that side of themselves in their next chapter of life.

In fact, there are elder programs that are looking to institutionalize ways to have retirees serve as mentors and trainers for entry level workers and even the middle career folks who could benefit from the wisdom of the experienced and senior people.

One woman I interviewed was looking to retire as a teacher and she suggested to the private school she worked in for more than 20 years that she would be available as a 'consultant' to mentor and train the new teachers. The school was delighted and realized how much expertise often walks out the door when their senior teachers retire. They are looking to create a program for all entry teachers to be matched with retired and retiring teachers perhaps 10 hours a week. This has proven to be an ideal situation for Julie and she enjoys sharing the skills she gained from years in the classroom.

This is a win-win for the school, the new teachers, and most of all, for the students.

Arlene—Realized She Loved the Dance

I interviewed Arlene a year before her long-awaited retirement as head of special services at a state university. Her career was satisfying. She had always been in academia in some capacity, supporting the deaf and blind community. Earlier in her career she had been a deaf interpreter. She loved what she thought of as doing a 'communications dance'. It had been tremendously rewarding work for her, and it made her feel alive and connected with her audience. But when she was promoted to department administrator, her focus was exclusively on budgets and contracts. She was no longer in touch with the communities she served. As an administrator she hired out that service through contractor agencies.

She really missed the deaf interpreting work. I suggested that perhaps she might contact the contract agencies and offer her services post retirement on a part time basis.

Her face lit up. Arlene got into action, reviewed her skills and was delighted when the contract agency took her on two days a week on a regular basis.

When we met six months later, Arlene was radiant. She was not only getting to do a part of her professional life she had long surrendered but was enjoying the work tremendously. Plus, the extra income allows her and her husband to take periodic long weekend vacations and provides some extras for their grown daughters and the grandchildren.

"It is time to step aside for a less experienced and less able person to take my place."

—Scott Elledge

Richard—Moves to the Mountains and Still Wants to Work

Richard and his wife were pleased to both be retiring in their early 60s. They set their sights on moving to the mountains and enjoying skiing on a regular basis. They felt that their retirement income could carry them.

But Richard still felt like he wanted to be of service and he missed the excitement of the emergency room. His wife, Nina, on the other hand, was looking forward to leaving her high stress business career and never wanted to work again. People are different.

Richard realized he had more 'juice' for his career and was excited at the prospect of working part time at a ski clinic where he could focus on winter sport injuries. He met with several medical centers and was delighted to find one that offered him just the part time commitment he was looking for. Similar to Mary, in the last example, he enjoyed both the work and having the extra income.

Steve the Finance Whiz

Steve spent 30 years in corporate finance, climbing the ranks by earning promotions that entailed additional responsibilities but with those responsibilities came more and more stress. The last five years of his tenure were a real 'countdown to freedom' as he put it. As he seriously considered his retirement years and fantasized about the wonders of freedom, he realized that it was the stress he was looking to escape.

The excitement and dynamic nature of the financial markets continued to fascinate him. So, he extracted the aspect of his work that would reflect that interest. Although his wife was surprised, he opted to spend about $600 a year on professional newsletters and resources that would keep him current on market developments and trends.

It is vital to do a careful review of your work or career life and capture those aspects that you enjoy and that add to the vitality of your life. I'm hoping that some of the examples spark your imagination and bring to mind things that you might like to extract and continue as you move forward in life.

Let's take a closer look.

YOUR TURN

1. What aspects of your work did you most enjoy? Think back to the various jobs you had starting early on. What skills do you feel you'll miss using? Are there new places you can take those skills?

_____

_____

_____

_____

_____

_____

2. What kind of research and calls can you make to find out where and how you can use those skills? Are there former colleagues who retired before you that you can consult with?

_____

_____

_____

_____

_____

_____

3. Are there new aspects of your work, or even extensions of your work, that you'd like to learn about? For instance, if you were a photographer, do you want to learn more about the new digital technologies?

_____

_____

_____

_____

_____

_____

CHAPTER FOUR

Your Life Force Never Retires

Time for personal growth

It's time to look at unfinished business. Yes, personal and psychological growth, including *Family Relations*: spouse, partner, siblings, cousins, parents, etc., both those with us, and those who've died but the relationship continues. It might include family issues you have been putting off because they are too painful or too complicated.

This was the most intriguing chapter for me to research and write. There is a lot currently written and researched about the power of getting to the bottom of things, righting wrongs, understanding one's life choices, processing one's hurts and pains. In fact, one author who became a hospice chaplain later in life wrote a book about her experiences with people in their final months and days. Most of them talked about their relationships, often family relationships and how they wished they had had the time to repair things and work on themselves.

As we approach our fourth quarter of life we can experience symptoms of fear, lethargy, depression, anxiety, and physical ailments. In the past, most people didn't live in good health long enough to face fourth-quarter challenges. But, lucky us, we are facing them and they offer an opportunity for resolution and peace.

"Knowing yourself is true wisdom. Mastering yourself is true power."

—Lao Tze

The Art of Being

During our career lives we are busy, sometimes super busy, with intense scheduling. We have a lot of responsibilities; our lives and calendars are full. We have our work lives, our family lives and often other responsibilities as well. When weekends come we want to enjoy ourselves, but also need to play catch up and take care of life maintenance tasks. That can take up most of the weekend. Yes, it is *doing doing doing*.

I'd like to suggest *The Fine Art of Being*, what I call the phenomena a number of retirees discussed with me. Each in their own words said something like 'You know, Joan, I now have the option of waking up sometimes and just staying in bed, reaching for the book on my nightstand and reading for an hour or two. Sometimes after lunch I just sit and think. I have time to reflect and things come up. In fact, I've even started a meditation class and love it. I love this new way of being. It is the art of being, exploring my own mind and thoughts. Getting more deeply in touch with myself. I never had a chance to explore my own thoughts and feelings like this before. I like slowing down sometimes and just *being*.'

Might you be accustomed to living life on the super-fast speed and like to slow down and try out a new, slower gear and perhaps tune into your life on a deeper level?

Loss and Renewal

Loss is inevitable in this winter stage of our lives.

This is also a time that deepens us as we lose dear friends and loved ones. Grief can be powerful, even overwhelming. We can get caught in it and have difficulty moving forward. This is a topic you might want to explore more deeply now that you will have more time.

When I experienced the deepest loss of my life, the death of my mother when I was 59 and she was 87, after a lifetime of true best friend relationship, I emotionally went to a depth of sadness and almost unreality I had never experienced before. It was frightening and I attribute the gift of a book, *Entering the Healing Ground* by Francis Weller, a psychotherapist specializes in grief work, to my ability to get through it.

Some people find the help they need in a support group and others might need to get personal counseling. By deeply processing our grief we can often emerge with renewed appreciation for the preciousness of our lives and those we love.

We also need to consider the spiritual and practical aspects of anticipating our own mortality.

Our Life Force Lives On

Our life force lives on in the lives of the people we have touched during our lifetime. The deepest imprint can be on our children, grandchildren and the generation that comes after ours.

Many of the people I met with for this book talked about the poignancy, importance and value of spending time with their grandchildren. They appreciate the time they now have to build deep bonds and share their interests, values and love. For those who don't have children or grandchildren, there are many children in this world who can benefit from the time and attention of special adults in their lives.

Self-Examination

If you can shape your life from the inside out, you can be fully alive with grace and passion. You will have a gift to give to yourself, your family, friends, community and to our world. There are many ways to explore

"This is the time to reimagine how to deal with places we feel stuck or trapped. This is the time to re-envision our failures and their true meaning. This is the time to expand our understanding of love and how love shapes our lives. This is the time to renew our vision of joy."

—Bud Harris

this opportunity to delve into your psychology, have the courage to see yourself clearly, and let your truths lead to further personal growth.

From my studies of personal and psychological development in the later decades I have learned that the topics we can include are:

- Imagining how to deal with places we feel stuck or trapped, deep fears that may have held us back
- Re-envisioning our failures, choices, their true meaning, and the possibilities they contain
- Expanding our understanding of love and how our deep relationships shape our lives from birth to death
- Restoring and renewing our vision of joy and living with enthusiasm and wonder
- Grappling with grief and our own eventual death

This exploration can be done in many ways:

1. Journaling and finding groups that do this work together to explore their deeper dimension
2. Considering counseling or psychotherapy if you realize there are some unresolved conflicts with important people in your life
3. Trying the Art of Being. Take up meditation, a live class or online study or even try a retreat
4. Trying yoga, tai chi or other more gentle forms of mind body exercise. Look for the classes for seniors or make sure it is a gentle and safe approach.
5. There are self-study books and tapes. See the *Further Resources* section at the end of the book
6. Elder groups
7. Memoir writing
8. Jumping in on your own to have discussions with family or the individuals with whom you have had issues

Steve—A Successful Business Man Who Realized He Was Sometimes a Bully

Steve owned and ran two businesses. He was an excellent provider for his family and he set up college funds for his children and grandchildren. He prided himself in his intelligence, leadership and business success.

However, he came to realize that he had caused pain to people along the way. He realized he had been impatient and sometimes mean and bullying.

He retired at 87 and decided to learn more about psychology on his own. He bought a comprehensive program from a top professor in psychology and studied a course on his own for over a year. He gained knowledge and insight. Though he still respected his career success, he realized he was sorry for the way he sometimes treated people. He realized he had caused pain to some of his employees and even to some family members.

He decided to write a letter to his children and grandchildren explaining that he would have been far more successful at work and in his personal life if he had learned to be more patient and kind. He recommended strongly that his children and grandchildren break the cycle and learn to value those important traits. He died at 89 years old knowing he had shared his deeper wisdom and made some needed apologies. He died with more peace and deeper connections to his family.

Karen—Finding her Biological Family

Karen was adopted at birth, grew up in a loving family, and had a wonderful life. She had a great education that put her on track for a successful career. Karen married and had her own children. All was well, but at the age of 60, when she and her husband were both facing retirement, her adoptive parents died. For the first time in her life she was curious to explore her roots.

Karen was motivated to learn more about her biological parents because she had some qualities and ways that were very different than from the family she grew up with. Now that her adoptive parents were no longer alive, she would not have to worry about hurting their feelings. She read up on the topic of adoptive family reunions, and knew to proceed cautiously.

She located and met with her biological mother and two half siblings. Karen made some important discoveries about herself. She not only got a better understanding of her characteristics, but over time, her own family benefitted from the inclusion of her biological relatives.

Valerie—Needed to Process Her Job Loss

Valerie was unfairly fired from the job she had planned to retire from. The employees at her company knew there was going to be a layoff, and one of her co-workers lied saying Valerie had said and done inappropriate things. Valerie's management believed her co-worker and she was fired.

She was devastated but advised not to fight back legally as it would be expensive, complicated, and difficult to prove. It took about a year, but Valerie did get a job at another company, but it was with lower pay and less responsibilities. Also, it did not provide the income she needed to fund her retirement until several years later.

When I met with Valerie, the anger was still fresh and strong. She was so upset by this unfairness that it had impacted many aspects of her life— her marriage and her health were deteriorating. She admitted she had become bitter and cynical and just couldn't seem to move forward.

Finally, her husband insisted they get counseling together and the counselor quickly saw that Valerie had been quite wounded and insisted on working with her in individual therapy.

It was a godsend. She hadn't realized the extent of pain and suffering she was experiencing and how it triggered other slights in her life and how powerfully it was destroying her relationships, health and her entire quality of life.

In therapy Valerie finally started to let go of her anger and started to heal, soften and release. She found a new depth of understanding, inner forgiveness and kindness coming back into her being.

She still knew she had been wounded but she re-framed her story and grew in compassion depth and forgiveness.

Before we get to YOUR TURN I'd like to share a quote from psychologist, Dr. Carl Jung, from the movie about him, *A Matter of Heart*.

"The great events of world history are, at bottom, profoundly unimportant. In the last analysis, the essential thing is the life of the individual. This alone makes history, here alone do the great transformations first take place, and the whole future, the whole history of the world ultimately springs as a giant summation from these hidden sources in individuals. In our most private and most subjective lives, we are not only the passive witnesses of our age, and its sufferers, but also its makers. We make our own epoch."

This quotation reminds us that each one of us is important. Each one of us can help change history and make life better. We need this new challenge of longer life head on, transforming and deepening ourselves and letting the results of these transformations flow into the world.

We don't need to move mountains to revolutionize the world. We just need to face our past, face our future and transform ourselves to be as free and vital as possible in our fourth quarter.

Will you take on that challenge?

EXERCISE

YOUR TURN

1. Looking honestly at your life, are there issues, conflicts or decisions you want to re-visit and better understand? How might you do that?

_____

_____

_____

_____

_____

_____

_____

2. What other opportunities for growth come to mind? Might you want to deepen your spiritual side—explore an organized religion or a spiritual path? Learn to meditate or slow down?

_____

_____

_____

_____

_____

_____

3. Explore your family relations. What's working well? Can you see room for improvement—more intimacy and deeper connection? Consider those most important to you: *spouse, partner, children, grandchildren, siblings, other family members. What steps might you take now that you have more time? Do any of these relationships need healing?*

This may be the perfect time to follow through on your intention to spend more with family. Some people establish weekly activities and visits to ensure vital times together. Some plan intergenerational vacations.

_____

_____

_____

_____

_____

_____

_____

_____

_____

4. Are there family members or other people you are estranged from or less close to now? Who are they? Think about re-establishing the bond.

_____

_____

_____

_____

_____

_____

_____

_____

_____

CHAPTER FIVE

Ya Gotta Have Friends

And social connections of all sorts

What would life be without friends to pal around with?

A sobering fact is that loneliness and isolation can be greater predictors of death than smoking or obesity. Our country is looking at social isolation as an epidemic problem in our upcoming decades as more and more older people leave the work force and are living alone.

Not good. We were not programmed for too much aloneness.

Some of us may be introverted and need to periodically have long periods of time alone, as my husband requires, but when we are ready to be social, we want people interaction. We need verification of our identity, preferences and interests.

We need others to reflect back who we are. Although family and especially spouses and partners play a key role in addressing intimacy, we still need what one of my favorite books, *Frientimacy* by Shasta Nelson refers to as *a heartfelt supportive closeness*.

Philosophers and cognitive scientists agree that friendship is an essential ingredient of human happiness. The way friendship enhances well-being, it turns out, has nothing to do with quantity and everything to do with quality. Researchers confirm that it isn't the number of friends (or, in the case of Facebook, "friends") we have, but the nature of those relationships.

"Good friends help you to find important things when you have lost them...your smile, your hope, and your courage."

—Doe Zantamata

"A friend knows the song in my heart and sings it to me when my memory fails."

—Donna Rober

In particular, what makes for a good happiness-enhancing friendship is the degree of companionship. When you do things together with your friend, you feel self-validation, when your friends reassure you that you are a good, worthy individual.

And as Dr. Bonior, author of *The Friendship Fix* wrote: "We don't have to go out and spend every minute of every day with a rotating cast of friends. It's about feeling like you are supported in the ways that you want to be supported and believing that the connections you do have are nourishing and strong."

In our careers we had built-in socializing with colleagues, associates, bosses, clients, and others. Although some of our work relationships were stressful at times, we were fully engaged socially so much so that many of us sought quiet time and alone time in our after-work hours.

In retirement, we are sometimes shockingly alone. Especially if our retirement coincides with the loss of our partner or loved one, or if we were always single, we really need to intentionally program social interaction into our lives. For some people, if they don't go out of the house for basics like groceries, and they live alone, they can truly face a depressing isolation.

We need to differentiate between the need for close friends and the need for social interaction in general. Studies show that people who live alone are far happier when they engage in daily small talk with their postal delivery person, supermarket clerk or bank teller, etc. My mother in her 80s, as her mobility decreased and her world got smaller, began establishing friendships with such people, even her landlord's family. They had their in-jokes and their time together was more than transactional; it was highly personal and rewarding for her.

Ellen's husband died shortly after he had retired, leaving her a widow at the age of 68. She noticed that the daily walks she used to have with her husband felt really lonely now. She joined a local walking club at her town's recreation center. She didn't particularly have a lot in common with the others, but she enjoyed the companionship and safety that walking in a group offered. It also picked up her pace and gave her a better workout.

So, it is time to dust off those friend-making skills. Whether it's to reignite friendships that fell away when we were too busy to feed them, or friends from years ago whom we now can connect with online. It is time to consciously look at expanding our friendship circle: for fun, engagement, interest and to feed our sense of connection.

Friends are critical to maintaining both physical and emotional health. Strong social ties boost the immune system and increase longevity. They also decrease the risk of contracting certain chronic illnesses and increase the ability to deal with chronic pain, according to a 2010 report in the Journal of Health and Social Behavior.

Just as we looked at extracting from our career life in Chapter 3, in terms of using our work-related skills, I'd like to suggest you look back at your career and think of some of the people you might want to continue to engage with outside of work. It's easier in some ways now that you are outside the political arena of the working world. Think of the colleagues you enjoyed sharing with on topics outside of work.

You can also spend time on the internet relating to friends far away. New research shows that a positive role that the internet can play is allowing socializing for older people who otherwise can't get out and about as much.

"Among older adults, relationships with friends are a better predictor of good health and happiness than relations with family."

—William Chopik

The internet is also a good way to find people with common interests. For people interested in certain activities like hiking, fishing, bird watching, etc. you can find special Meet Up groups online that are near to you geographically.

Caroline—Found Connection by Seeking Out a Local Book Club

Caroline had a long career in accounting in a large company. By nature, she was introverted and spent a lot of time reading and enjoying her pets. She always had one or two close friends but when she and her husband moved to be closer to her aging mother, she had no friends in her new community.

> "Let us be grateful to people who make us happy, they are the charming gardeners who make our souls blossom."
>
> —Marcel Proust

Forlorn, she finally realized that she needed to reach out to find just the kind of women she enjoyed being around…readers. It happened that at her neighborhood annual potluck she told people what she was seeking. She was introduced to a neighbor who had started a book club and invited her to her join.

Caroline got intentional, not only about increasing her social life, but she thought through the specific kinds of interests she wanted. Having a monthly book club and periodic lunches with a couple of the women she met is fully engaging her need for social life and friendship.

Dennis—Finds Fellow Fans at a Sports Bar

Dennis retired from years as a city planner in California. His work years were hectic and he was in meetings most of the day. He thought he was focused almost exclusively on work topics but looking back he realized that a highlight of his time with colleagues was discussing sporting events: the big football games, basketball championships, and tennis matches.

Once retired, he really missed that jovial and spirited interaction about sports. His wife and family did not share his passion for spectator sports.

But he found that a favorite local southern food restaurant had a sports bar attached. When he heard the cheers and shout-outs he realized that he had found the crowd he wanted to be with. He was not much of a drinker but could nurse a beer for the game and loved meeting with like-minded sports guys at the bar.

Julie—Still Worked as a Realtor but Missed Dear Friends Who Passed

"Many people will walk in and out of your life but only true friends leave footprints in your heart."

—Eleanor Roosevelt

Julie was a successful realtor who had worked hard as a single mother to provide for herself and her three children after her husband died in his 30s.

When her children completed college, she sold the family home and downsized to a less expensive condo. She was saddened as her closest two women friends, also single moms, had both passed away in the last two years.

She and her adult children recognized she was sinking into a depression, but she had an idea that she decided to act on.

She posted a note on her community online bulletin board saying she was interested in finding walking partners for two to three mornings a week. That is how she met two women, also single, about her age. Over time they not only walked together but found other mutually satisfying activities like movie going and potluck dinners.

Yes, ya gotta have friends: old friends, new friends, friends to share activities, intimate friends, and even online friends to chat with. The importance of friendship is being recognized more and more. In Britain they have even appointed a Minister for Loneliness. There are two excellent books on friendship in the Further Resources section.

I strongly recommend you take some time to think about the questions below that will prompt you to take a serious look at your social situation.

EXERCISE

YOUR TURN

1. Reflect on your social life. Are you happy with the quality and quantity of friends and social interactions in your life? Please describe

_____

_____

_____

_____

_____

2. Do you have friends you can really talk to about personal and even private matters, that you can call in a time of need? Do you have people to call for activities you want to do? Do you have local friends whom you can call to see a movie, take a walk, eat a meal together, go on a trip with?

_____

_____

_____

_____

_____

3. Do you want to deepen or change any of your current friendships? Are there any friendships that are not serving you that you'd like to end? How will you go about it? How can you enhance or expand your social sphere?

_____
_____
_____
_____
_____

4. If your world is changing anticipate how you would like your social life to look. Write down your thoughts and desires. Now that you'll have more time, do you want to re-connect and catch up with old friends? Who are they? Do you want to increase the frequency and or depth of current friends? Do you want to reach out to find new friends?

_____
_____
_____
_____
_____

5. Would it enhance your life to explore community or group activities where you'll have common interests? Would you enjoy finding a book club, card group, political group, exercise group, faith community, etc.?

_____
_____
_____
_____
_____

Service,
Community,
Legacy

Giving back

Service

6

How will you leave the world a better place?

What do you want to be remembered for?

What legacy will you leave?

First Off, Why Do It?

The simple answer is: it feels good, it feels right. It just feels good to be of use and helpful to others. We are wired this way. We seem to have an altruism gene. Additionally, the closer the activity and the people you help are aligned with your personal passions and interests, the better you will feel and the more impact you will have.

There are also health reasons. Our hearts really are happier and our systems function better when we know we are being of use to others and to our world. In fact, when I interviewed people for this book, at least 80 percent of them talked about community service, volunteering or mentorship work as a significantly fulfilling part of their lives. The 20 percent that did not mention it, responded positively when I brought it up. They just didn't know how or where to get involved. Once I gave them some ideas they were ready to go.

Research supports the idea of giving back and enlarging your world. If people feel they are making a difference, they are happier. In an article by Jenny Santi for Time Magazine, I read that science is starting to prove

"Anyone who thinks they are too small to make a difference has never tried to fall asleep with a mosquito in the room."

—Christine Todd Whitman

this. Santi wrote: "Through MRI technology, we now know that giving activates the same parts of the brain that are stimulated by food and sex. Experiments show evidence that altruism is hardwired in the brain—and it's pleasurable. *Helping others may just be the secret to living a life that is not only happier but also healthier, more productive, and meaningful.*"

A study published in BMC Public Health concluded that taking time to volunteer—by serving in a soup kitchen or reading to others—could reduce early mortality rates by 22 percent, compared with those who did not volunteer.

As we look into our later years we often go deeper and think about the meaning and impact of our lives on others. In Chapter Four we looked at the meaning and impact we have via our relationships with our family and in Chapter Five we looked at our friendships, but this chapter is about our impact on the broader world. How can we offer up our talents, skills, personalities, time and attention?

The other advantage of volunteer work is that it can provide structure in one's life that some people crave once they leave their workplace. When one has a full-time job it often feels too demanding and too structured but when retirement comes, it's 24/7 unstructured. One can feel untethered and unmoored. By setting up a regular schedule, what I call 'anchor points' in the week, you can have predictability and just enough structure in your life.

What Might You Enjoy Doing for Others and for Your Community?

I caught the give-back bug early on. I spent every Wednesday afternoon volunteering in a local daycare center for low income children. I did it because I enjoyed it so much. It was completely absorbing and great fun. I realized then how much I enjoyed engaging with children.

What started as a one-day experience extended to a four-year run that provided me sweet memories of my high school years.

It was giving back. It was giving my time and attention to children who needed and longed for attention. It was great for the kids but it was also meaningful and worthwhile to me. In contrast to the angst and complexity of teen relationships, this was pure, simple and joyful.

It was an activity that has been a part of my life to this day. I expanded on my time with children and now do both literacy and art instruction one afternoon a week with second and third graders. At the end of my life I will reflect back on the memories. I will enjoy the wonderful pictures and letters the children write to me at year end and see their smiling faces in my mind.

In my interviews with retired people I learned that often a highlight of their time is their volunteer work, their time of being of service. The more the activity and audience really spoke to them, the more meaningful the activity.

Susan, whom you met in Chapter One, the avid skier, is now volunteering with a wounded veterans' group that gives the injured veterans a chance to enjoy time out on the slopes. Accommodations are made to their special requirements. Susan says that although it is physically taxing work, it is tremendously fulfilling to see their satisfaction, enjoyment, and sense of freedom and fun as they engage together going downhill.

Natalie is dedicating herself to the homeless in her city. For years she sat on a board dedicated to the homeless in her community. Now retired, she has the time to get out on to the streets to give direct help which she finds much more satisfying. Each winter she works with a team to distribute blankets, hats, socks and warm beverages to the homeless. She said that not only has this work been satisfying but the

"The true meaning of life is to plant trees, under whose shade you do not expect to sit."

—Nelson Mandela

connections she makes to both her co-workers and to some of the homeless people, has been life changing. She feels a deeper sense of gratitude for her own circumstances, and a profound realization of her connection to all people. She discussed with me her ever-growing spirituality that comes from this work. Natalie added that with her increased focus on helping others she naturally works harder to keep herself in good health, aware of the need to stay strong for her work on the streets.

Charlene was a professional nurse and having always been single, she felt that the best retirement for her would be joining the Red Cross and being trained to go as needed to emergencies around the world. She has been doing that for the last 10 years and it has expanded her world view, friendships, and sense of meaningful contribution.

Social and Political Action

Many people have strong political and social views, but haven't had the time to express them due to the demands of career and family. But now, with the gift of time, you might think of ways to be active in the larger political and social arena. Many churches, synagogues and mosques offer social and political action opportunities that might give you a way to get involved with others in a meaningful way for causes you believe in.

Bill—A Retired Doctor, Goes Back to Work

Bill had a very busy practice as a surgeon and retired at 70. He and his wife had plans to travel the world, after putting off vacations for decades due to work and family obligations, but stuff happens.

Bill's wife died just six months after he retired. He was devastated and spent a year in grief and mourning.

Then he was asked to visit a local non-profit medical clinic in the hopes he might have a couple of hours a week to volunteer. He went, but reluctantly, as he was fighting depression and not feeling particularly energized. Well, you might guess the rest.

Bill ended up not only spending more and more time at the clinic taking care of low income patients, but over time, he ended up becoming the clinic director and playing a very active role in community outreach for fundraising.

Bill moved to Plan B in his life. The money he and his wife had set aside for travel was now going to the clinic, and he was feeling he had expanded his life but in different ways than travel would have afforded him.

Bill also made a lot of new friends at the clinic and his social life took on a new form, a very satisfying one.

Pat—A Master Gardener Devotes Her Energies to Rescue Animals and Abused Children

Pat had been a high school teacher for 30 years and welcomed the chance to spend hours and hours tending her garden. For decades she had spent weekends in gardening classes and finally earned a master gardener certification.

"The needs of the person are the needs of the planet; the needs of the planet are the needs of the person."

—Theodore Roszak

One day, just a few months after retiring, she met a woman at a social gathering who ran a non-profit farm just outside of her town that brought rescue animals and abused children together in a program for healing. They needed help with their gardens and wanted to construct a special cemetery for pets. Pat was asked to help.

She thought she'd help to set up the program and then return to her home garden, but the more she got involved with the farm, the more opportunities she saw to contribute. Her educational background ended up being ideal for their programming with teens and her work at the farm expanded to be a three-times-a-week effort.

Pat couldn't be happier.

Jane and Dennis—Create a Scholarship

Jane was a corporate trainer and Dennis was a financial advisor. When they met in their early 40s, they discovered they had the same vision of hoping to someday build a college scholarship for low income, worthy students.

Each of them had worked several jobs to put themselves through college and graduate school and they knew the toll that took. They wanted to give back by being able to fund a four-year scholarship for a deserving student. So, when they retired, they prioritized their retirement income and allotted a certain amount of money each year for such a scholarship.

They worked with a local high school to set up their program and now have the joy of interviewing and selecting a student every four years with whom they meet monthly for encouragement and mentoring. This form of give back creates a legacy of compassion and philanthropy that is satisfying to them and sets a fine example to their children.

Now let's look at ways you might want to incorporate volunteer work, being of service, and giving back. Let's explore what kind of legacy you'd like to leave.

 **YOUR TURN**

1. Have you done volunteer work in the past that you found meaningful? What did you do and is that the kind of work you would like to do now?

_____

_____

_____

_____

2. Are there the issues in our world that you'd like to become involved with? For example: hunger, education, healthcare, the environment, the arts, politics, faith, literacy, other?

_____

_____

_____

3. Do you have skills and talents you want to use and contribute now? This could include your career related skills, hobbies, sports, etc.

_____

_____

_____

4. Are there ways you'd like to give back with your spouse, partner or other friends or family? Is there a discussion you'd like to have with them on this topic of legacy and volunteerism?

_____

_____

_____

5. Imagine you have died and you are listening to someone talk about your positive impact on the world. What would you like to hear them say?

_____

_____

_____

_____

CHAPTER SEVEN

The *NEW*

Come let's explore

The *NEW*! What do you now have time to explore...travel, classes, politics or new hobbies?

Yes, it is time to embrace the New. It is time to be creative and open up to new possibilities. It is time to really be excited that you have reached this stage in your life where your responsibilities are covered, your health and vibrancy are still strong and you have the TIME to explore for no other reason than pure enjoyment and enrichment.

For some folks, retirement can be too wide open and too expansive an opening. For others, it is happy-time and they are working off a mile-long bucket list that they started years ago. I encourage you to at least consider a road not taken before as it might take you to destinations that enliven and add to your sense of fun and meaning.

If you have a spouse or partner, it's fun to build this plan with them or even with your extended family or close friends. Many couples I met with enhanced their connection to one another by experiencing new things together. I heard delightful accounts of multi-generational trips and experiences involving adult children and grandchildren. They made sure to accommodate the needs of all age groups.

Think of aspects of the 'essential you' that you would love to further develop.

"Everyone has a 'risk muscle'. You keep it in shape by trying new things. If you don't, it atrophies. Try to use your 'risk muscle' daily!"

—Roger von Oech

In meeting with about 100 people for this book, those who were most excited and happily engaged in their retirement or planning for it, showed curiosity and openness to the NEW. They intentionally decided to explore new interests, hobbies, travels and activities. They intentionally chose activities that were beyond the familiar.

"It is never too late to be what you might have been."

—George Eliot

Some were engaged in new hobbies, learning new languages, developing skills to volunteer in new ways, teaching classes or taking classes on new subjects. A popular class for those over 55 is memoir writing—gaining perspective, reflecting on one's life, sharing insights and wisdom with others. Many colleges are now offering classes in memoir writing.

Elder Gifts

Another new thing to explore are Elder Circles as described at www.sage-ing.org. These Sage-ing Elder Circles or Elder Gift Circles are where seniors are learning to embrace and acknowledge their inner gifts gleaned from decades of living. These gifts can be emotional, spiritual, physical, intellectual or psychological. In these circles you identify and learn how to share and integrate your gifts with others. You see examples of this in mixed aged communities where young children and seniors do activities together, befitting both age groups. You see it with senior mentors advising high school students on life lessons and career directions. Rather than absorbing popular culture's message about elders' lack of significance and fading external looks, they are going deeper to reconnect with many cultures which have valued the experience and wisdom of their elders. How wonderful to connect with the gifts you have, to give to the world of tomorrow.

Elder seminars are often taught at community centers and houses of faith.

Learning for the Joy of It

Many universities and colleges are recognizing that older adults have learning needs, too. They may not be motivated by achieving credentials or advanced degrees, but purely for the joy of expanding their lives and keeping in touch with the larger world. Osher Lifelong Learning Institutes www.osherfoundation.org have set up programs at many campuses and they often attract top professors and the classes do not require grades, tests or papers. Other universities, colleges and junior colleges often have community learning centers and offer classes at reduced tuition for seniors.

The Creative Arts

Involvement with the creative arts was mentioned quite often by the people I interviewed for this book. Many were looking forward to finally have the time to attend theater, concerts, opera and dance performances. Several looked forward to being able to leisurely explore art galleries and museums. Some were excited to learn and express themselves through art forms: painting, drawing, sculpting, playing instruments, learning to sing, etc. The most enthusiastic were those diving into a new form of expression.

Keeping Up with Advances in Health

As we age we are concerned with our health. The Buck Institute in California is focused on "biomedical advances aimed at altering the aging process to prevent, delay or cure chronic diseases". It is a fascinating institute and you can keep up with their developments at www.buck-insitute.org. We need to take ownership of keeping up with medical, health and lifestyle research to do all we can to stay vital. Use the magic of the Google search to find good resources known universities and medical centers. Do check on the reliability of the information you find.

"Once we believe in ourselves, we can risk curiosity, wonder and spontaneous delight, for new experiences reveal our unique human spirit."

—ee cummings

Starting Over in a New Location—Even a New Lifestyle

When you are no longer tethered to a career with a specific workplace, or to raising a family, your options for where and how to live can expand. Some retirees opt to move to lower cost areas. Others look for new ways to live, including communal situations where resources are shared and social interaction is encouraged. You might want to explore new ways of living if you're newly single or have a spouse with health problems. Just because you've always lived a certain way doesn't mean you have to continue that lifestyle or place. Be open to exploring! Take a look at *How we Live Now; Redefining Home and Family in the 21st Century* by Bella DePaulo, listed in Further Resources.

Let's look at some individuals who have embarked on the NEW.

Emily and Ted—Traveling, But in a New Way

Over the years, Emily and Ted always chose group travel experiences as that gave them efficient use of time. The research was always done for them.

But in retirement they decided to travel a new way. Now the internet provides a multitude of travel resources and information. You can have a lot of fun researching. Trip Advisor and many other travel blogs and travel sites, along with Air BnB, VRBO, provide the world at your finger-tips. Emily and Ted thought it might be fun to design their own trips and go solo.

They took a class at a local college about planning a trip to Italy. It inspired them to take a class called Italian for Travelers together. They planned a month-long trip to Italy, off season, staying in Air BnBs, taking trains, going to local markets and cooking their own meals. They enjoyed planning the trip together as much as the trip.

This was new territory and their learning curve was steep. But it was tremendously gratifying and romantic They ended up meeting new people as they traveled, and felt they really tasted and enjoyed a new culture. They plan to continue with independent traveling for as long as they can.

Maggie—Turning a Hobby into a New and Unexpected Second Career

Maggie always saw herself as a serious student, coming to the US with her husband for him to pursue his career while she completed her PhD. She hunkered down to work as a scientist throughout her career. Her husband left her shortly after their child was born and she focused on raising their daughter and working hard. She prospered both as a mother and as a career professional.

At 65 she was able to fully retire and finally gave herself a chance for fun. She had always loved photography and nature travel, but both interests had been limited due to her responsibilities.

It was her sister who suggested she build a small travel and photography business. She reminded Maggie of her commitment to animals and habitat preservation and suggested a percentage of her profit could go to animal sanctuaries. At first Maggie balked, but her sister encouraged her to think about the idea.

Maggie took the plunge. She spent a few years learning and focusing on nature photography and then set up a small tour group taking others on photo expeditions. For the first time she was doing something she truly loved.

"The most regretful people on earth are those who felt the call to creative work, who felt their own creative powers restive and uprising, and gave to it neither power nor time."

—Mary Oliver

Shirley—Never Too Late to be a Ham!

Shirley was tall and skinny and never felt particularly attractive. She was happy to marry young, have four sons and put her energies into raising them. When her husband died in his early 60s she decided to try on new ways of being.

For the first time in her life, in her mid-70s she started to appreciate and enjoy her appearance. Finally, she felt pretty; her tallness and thinness were now considered attractive.

She shocked her sons by auditioning to be in television commercials. She was referred to an agent who saw her potential, styled her, and put her in front of the right people and the right opportunities. She not only felt great but also had a nice and unexpected secondary income.

What can you imagine might be THE NEW for you? How can you flex your RISK MUSCLE?

EXERCISE ▶ **YOUR TURN**

1. Dream Enter your bucket list or some things you know already that you want to do. What are they? If you don't have a bucket list, please stretch your imagination and brainstorm things that sound fun and enlivening to you. List them here.

_____

_____

_____

_____

_____

_____

2. What else might be the NEW for you? How else can you flex your Risk Muscle?

_____

_____

_____

_____

3. Review your answers in Chapter Three. What interests, talents or passions were revealed? Are there ones you want to further explore now?

_____

_____

_____

_____

4. Explore the people dimension. The NEW can involve people you might know but haven't had the opportunity to get to know well. Perhaps a trip with a special cousin or brother. Perhaps a reunion.

_____

_____

_____

_____

5. The physical dimension. So many people feel they are out of shape because they just don't have time to exercise. Well, now you have that time. Might you want to get in condition to go on a bike trip? A hiking trip? Set the goal of a half marathon? Think Active, think NEW. A sport that several people mentioned to me in our interviews was Pickleball.

_____

_____

_____

_____

CHAPTER EIGHT

Building an Action Plan

For your *NEW* retirement!

Congratulations! You've done a lot of important work. You've read and completed all seven of the building block chapters. This last chapter is where you pull it together into an Action Plan.

This is your personal roadmap for an intentional and multi-faceted future. Imagine a full and rich life for yourself that includes enjoying time with your loved ones, taking care of your mind and body and feeling good by giving back.

Action Plan building is a two-part process: first completing the graphic, and then write out your plan with specifics and due dates. We are building in accountability to make sure your plan goes from intention to reality!

YOUR TURN

1. **A visualization exercise**: Imagine you have an unscheduled week ahead. Please think for a few minutes about what you are most looking forward to doing with that precious gift of time. You might repeat ideas from earlier chapters in the book, and that is fine. I just want you to have a chance to anticipate yourself full activated, and choosing *intention* and *meaning* and *fun*!

"Everyone is a house with four rooms, a physical, a mental, an emotional, and a spiritual. Most of us tend to live in one room most of the time but unless we go into every room every day, even if only to keep it aired, we are not a complete person.'

—Indian proverb

EXERCISE

"Every journey of a thousand miles starts with one step."

—Lao Tze

2. Review and transfer your pertinent intentions, notes and responses from each of the chapters you participated in, plus question #1 above. Put that information in the building block graphic provided.

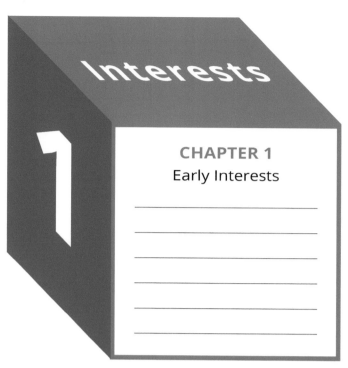

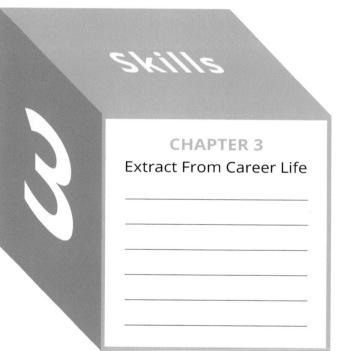

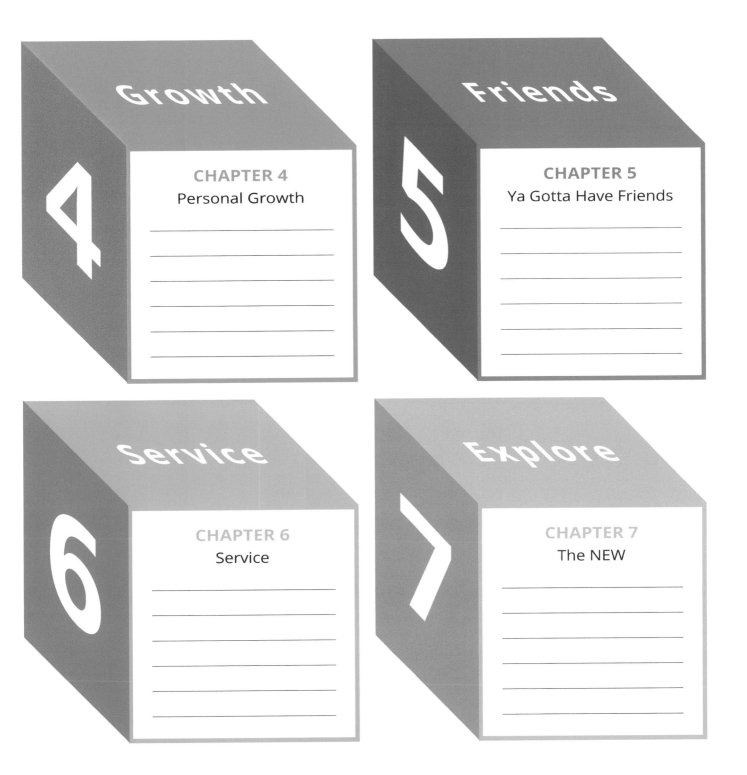

Growth

4

CHAPTER 4
Personal Growth

_____

_____

_____

_____

_____

Friends

5

CHAPTER 5
Ya Gotta Have Friends

_____

_____

_____

_____

_____

Service

6

CHAPTER 6
Service

_____

_____

_____

_____

_____

Explore

7

CHAPTER 7
The NEW

_____

_____

_____

_____

_____

3. Please complete your Action Plan as much as possible, on the next page. Make sure to add specifics and dates as that will encourage you to really get going!

Action Plan

Name _____

Intention/Activity	Interim Steps	Start Date

Intention/Activity	Interim Steps	Start Date

Further Resources

This Chair Rocks: A Manifesto Against Ageism, Ashton Applewhite

The Second Half of Life: Opening the Eight Gates of Wisdom, Angles Arrien

Younger Next Year: Live Strong, Fit, and Sexy Until You're 80 and Beyond, Chris Crowley and Henry S. Lodge, M.D.

How We Live Now: Redefining Home and Family in the 21st Century, Bella DePaulo

On Living, Kerry Egan

I Feel Bad About My Neck and Other Thoughts on Being a Woman, Nora Ephron

The December Project: An extraordinary rabbi and a skeptical seeker confront life's greatest mystery, Sarah Davidson

Friendfluence: The Surprising Ways Friends Make Us Who We Are, Carlin Flora

Aging Strong: The Extraordinary Gift of a Longer Life, Bud Harris, Ph.D.

Disrupt Aging: A Bold New Path To Living Your Best Life at Every Age, Jo Ann Jenkins

Friendtimacy: How to Deepen Friendships for Lifelong Health and Happiness, Shasta Nelson

Conscious Living Conscious Aging: Embrace and Savor Your Next Chapter, Ron Pevny

Still Here: Embracing Aging, Changing, and Dying, Ram Dass

Happy Retirement and the Psychology of Reinvention: A practical guide to planning and enjoying the retirement you've earned,
Kenneth S. Shultz, PhD

From Age-ing to Sage-ing: A Revolutionary Approach to Growing Older, Zalman schacher-Shalomi and Ronald S. Miller

Entering the Healing Ground: Grief, Ritual and the Soul of the World, Francis Weller

www.Intentionalretirement.com

www.aarp.com

www.sage-ing.org

Volunteer Ideas

FeedingAmerica.org

Hunger Relief—You can find local food banks in almost every town and city in the United States.

HumaneSociety.org

Animal Services—the largest and most effective animal protection agency. Their web site can help you to locate a local site where you can volunteer.

NPS.gov

National Park Service—They are always looking for volunteers. They provide training, hard work and fun in our beautiful national parks.

PeaceCorps.gov

Peace Corps—If you're up for adventure and hands-on, grass roots driven volunteer work worldwide. Of note is that over 5% of their volunteers are over the age of 50.

Elderwisdomcircle.org

You will find these wisdom circles all over the USA and they are designed to help you appreciate your later years, identify your unique gifts and find ways to share and use them in your life.

Habitat.org

Habitat for Humanity—a non-profit that builds simple and affordable housing for people who need shelter. Our President Jimmy Carter has been involved with them for decades, doing hands on building even in his 80s!

VolunteerForever.com

Volunteer Vacations, also known as Voluntourism and Voluntours or Road Scholar (formerly EdlerHostel)—combine travel and service with education.

VolunteerMatch.org

Volunteer Matching— Find local opportunities to volunteer in a full range of causes in your community. Programs range from senior foster grand-parenting to providing business skills to supporting homebound seniors.

CasaforChildren.org

What Is CASA? CASAs (Court Appointed Special Advocates) are volunteers and ordinary citizens, like you, doing extraordinary work. CASA advocates establish stable relationships with foster children, getting to know their unique history and making informed recommendations to the courts.

Score.org

SCORE is the nation's largest network of volunteer, expert business mentors, with more than 10,000 volunteers in 300 chapters. As a resource partner of the U.S. Small Business Administration (SBA), SCORE has helped more than 10 million entrepreneurs through mentoring, workshops and educational resources for over 50 years.

You can also go to the **AARP.org** web site for additional volunteer ideas for seniors. Or, get off your computer and visit your local library, school, religious institution, or political campaign office. Meet the locals and see how you can participate!

Acknowledgements

I could not have written Building Blocks for the NEW Retirement, or made it half as interesting and real, without the discussions with all of the people interviewed for this book. They are an especially vital group of individuals; every meeting was enriching and expanded my thinking. As people discussed their next stage of life, they were candid, vulnerable, impressive, funny, poignant, sad and creative. They were authentic and real, sharing their personal stories and discoveries with me, and I had the privilege of sharing them with you.

Thank you, to all of you who contributed to the texture and shape to this new period of revitalment vs retirement. I enjoyed the opportunity of sharing with you and listening to your personal stories. You injected vibrancy and realism into the building block model presented in this book. Naturally, I changed names and specifics to ensure confidentiality.

And a huge thank you to Andrea Granahan—my editor, friend, cheer leader, laughing partner and keeper of the schedule. Thank you dear Andrea for your skills, your commitment to this project, and your encouragement for me to make this book the best I possibly could.

I extend a huge thank you and much appreciation to Lauren Smith, the inestimable designer and graphic communicator who never fails to delight me with his work. Lauren understands the impact of clear and beautiful graphics and design to make a book like this accessible and enjoyable to read and participate in. He and I have worked together for over 25 years on many projects, and I hope we have many more projects together in the future.

I also want to thank my dear, sweet husband, David, who always shows tremendous patience and support as he sees me retreat to my office for many, many hours at a time. David, you are my love, my anchor, and I wish you a retirement with meaning, purpose, fun and...me!

Author Page

Joan Tabb is a coach, consultant, author, columnist and public speaker. She lives in Santa Rosa, California, an hour north of San Francisco, with her husband, David and their two dogs.

Joan is the founder and principal of Great in 8 Coaching, guiding clients to successfully launch, transition and advance in their careers. She is known to many as Coach Joan from both her practice and weekly blog, *Dear Coach Joan: Career Advice*.

Prior to coaching, Joan led a 20 year leadership career, building award-wining sales training for Memorex and Apple, then moving to 3Com where she managed global marketing communication programs. Joan then caught the start-up bug and successfully led marketing communications for several new ventures including Com21.

Joan, as an expert in transitions, realized that she and her Baby Boomer peers are facing a new phase of longer life, with years of vitality in front of them. Thus emerged the idea for *Building Blocks for the NEW Retirement*.

Her first book *Great in 8: Job Seeking Skills* enabled hundreds of job seekers to get back to work after the recession, and continues to be relevant.

Joan earned her BA cum laude in Psychology from the University of Pennsylvania and after three years in advertising and public relations in New York City moved to the west coast where she earned her MA in Instructional design at the University of Oregon. She then moved to Silicon Valley for career opportunities.

Outside of work, Joan enjoys doing volunteer literacy and art projects with children, participating in *Impact100*, a local women's philanthropy group, hiking, yoga, and keeping up with her reading for two book clubs.

Joan hopes that you found *Building Blocks for the NEW Retirement* to be useful, even inspiring. She appreciates you taking the time to post a positive review on Amazon.com so others can learn about it.

Joan is available to consult, coach or speak about the NEW Retirement, life transitions, and career topics.

Contact Joan Tabb at: Joan@Greatin8Coaching.com

Web site: www.Greatin8Coaching.com

Notes

CPSIA information can be obtained
at www.ICGtesting.com
Printed in the USA
LVHW02n0600170418
573735LV00002B/2/P